AF595394

KINTSUGI BY HADNI is the property of RLFPA Editions (OPC) Pvt Ltd — an imprint of RædLeaf Foundation for Poetry & Allied Arts (since 2012), not-for-profit, an independent literary organization committed to promoting poetry and allied arts in India and abroad.

First Publication Date: February 2020
ISBN: 978-81-939295-8-2
₹300 | US $9.99
Originally Published in Paperback
Cover Design: Linda Ashok

Manufactured in India, published & funded
by RLFPA Editions (OPC) Pvt Ltd.

INTRODUCTION

Ra Sh (N Ravi Shanker) is a much revered Indian English poet, translator, short-story and scriptwriter from Pallakad, Kerala. Author of two volumes of poetry: *Architecture of Flesh*, and *The Bullet Train and Other Loaded Poems*, Ra Sh's poetry is available in German and French translations.

RaSh has been a significant contributor to South Indian literature as a translator. His works include-

Biography
Mother Forest by C.K. Janu, Kerala tribal leader

Poetry Anthologies
Waking is another Dream (Sri Lankan Tamil resistance poems)
How to Translate an Earthworm (an anthology of 101 contemporary Malayalam poems)

Essays
Kochiites by Bony Thomas on the migrant communities in Kochi

Short Stories
Harum-Scarum Saar and Other Stories by Bama, Tamil Dalit writer,
Don't Want Caste by Malayalam Dalit writers
Ichi Tree Monkey and Other Stories (upcoming)

English Subtitlist
A dozen feature films in Malayalam and Tamil.

You can connect with this phenomenal person at shankeran@gmail.com.

At RLFPA EDITIONS, we are very proud to represent his voice.

KINTSUGI BY HADNI

POEMS

CONTENTS

DEATH SHOWS ME SNOW

When death came for me,
I asked *him* to carry me
(*him,* not *her,* death isn't a female)
through snow, not fire.

Have you never seen snow?
he asked [with pity]
I said, "have seen ice on sticks,
in cups, as slabs, hailstorms,
cubes, nuts, and as frozen fisheyes.
never snow."

So, death passed me
through a glass tube to where it snowed always
all my beloved ones watched me—
I travelled in style through glassy snow

I realized that snow was just frozen sperms;
they broke through frozen ova and formed
frozen zygotes till the tube warmed up
heated to impossible temperatures
akin to several suns

When the tube-ride ended,
we were thrown into a viscous ocean
that rumbled and yawned in
the pangs of creation.

When i woke up in the hospital bed,
I was surrounded by evolving creatures—
they sweetly sang a requiem for me, so sweet
that my eyes brimmed over with distilled remorse

I asked them who they were?
they cried [in unison],
'DEATH!'

CORRIDOR OF LOVE

Stalking the shadow, I feel her presence,
of the one who walked here before.

This is the Corridor of Love
    Majestic loves that wilted in marriage
    Pathetic ones that ended in suicide
    Inarticulate ones that failed to take off
    Violent ones that ended in bloodshed

Rich ones, Poor ones, Literate ones, Illiterate ones,
Urban ones, Rural ones, Pre-marital ones, Post-marital ones,
Extra-marital ones, Incestuous ones, Immoral ones,
        Inter-caste, Inter-religious, Inter-culture,
        Carnal, Platonic, Homemade,
Forced ones, Adolescent ones, Mature ones,
Gay ones, Lesbian ones, Transgender ones,
Polygamous ones, Polyandrous ones, Polyamorous ones,
        Sensual, Bestial, Hardcore, Soft-core,
        Made-in-Heaven, Made-in-Hell.

All assemble here in this Corridor of Love
to record their history on walls, lips, and bodies.

Here, I am stalking the shadow of my love-

She who walked here before I walked
She who blossomed before I did
She who swam in this green pond before me
She who dragged me by my phallus
        and laid down rules for me to follow,
        rules of love to be unbroken forever
She who minted the coins I exchange
She who etched the words I scrawl
She who tuned my throat and toned my muscles
She who constructed me bone by bone.

If I don't find her shadow now,
I have to flay my skin and rip my flesh for my love to gush out.
I know she will come before I am drained.
    For, if I cease to exist
        she ceases too
        so does this Corridor*

*In the Hill Palace Museum, Trippunithura, I walked a corridor where lovers thronged. Pseudo-moral Kerala drives its lovers to shadowy corridors to pursue their love.

KINTSUGI BY HADNI

Cannot deny that I have a brittle heart—
weak and fragile, thin like ice.

As it happens with hearts that are volleyed
back and forth,
mine too drops and cracks—
crunch like a bag of wafers.

Now, you know that girls make the best cardiologists.
The *heart* is their medium—their crystal ball;
they can gaze at it
and stir up storms.

So, every time my *heart* breaks,
I take it to another girl.

One girl squeezed out the blood,
washed it with peroxide, &
dried it before pinning it
with safety pins.

Another, pumped it with distilled water,
rinsed it with prill and spirit to
bind it all together
with a thick stapler.

The third one, weighed &
measured it—
blew hot air, to check for holes
Later, she masterfully
stitched it
with a gunny bag machine.

The last one was precise and trim—
she took my semen
mixed it &
plastered it in gold and blood.

But, once again, my heart goes *phut*—
I feel it from the thud of the pulse.

Now I hear of a tribal girl named Hadni—
in the valley of Buzzanooks
—who can mend any broken heart
with the sap of the Merjalinna flower,
the menstrual blood of the third moon
mixed with the pollen of Grzychterumb,
volcanic ash of the misty mountain
of Nettttzzzkkkppoo & the juice of *Bahmabah*

I wonder whether
she has a customer care number
toll free.

METAMORPHOSIS

She said, "Look,
all the fish have turned into rocks."

I saw   water
I saw   the trees in the water
I saw   the clouds in the trees in the water
I saw   a spaceship in the clouds in the trees in the water

People crossed the river on foot
A battle tank rolled across crushing the stones
A lizard scurried across to the other bank
Silence and darkness settled over the river

There were no people now
        No lizards.
                No tanks.
                        No ships

We stood on opposite banks
Watching each other melting into the night

We heard the roar of the waters
    gushing from the hills—
        the river rolling in a war-cry

We swam towards each other
The rocks around us came to life
They had turned into fish

                We too.

The first two lines are from the Korean film 'Once upon a summer.'

WITH APOLOGIES TO KAMALA DAS

I loved in five languages
Made love in four
Dreamt in three

One made me her master
    asked me to flog her
        with a horsetail whip
Her blood was honey.

One made me her slave
    Peed all over me that
        I licked my body clean
Her pee was nectar.

One made me her son
    Breastfed me
        I drank to my fill.
Her milk was ambrosia.

One made me her dad
    Asked me to tuck her in.
        I read stories to her.
Her finger was abloom.

One made me her friend
Went fishing together
I caught a whale, & she, a shark
I ate the shark, and she, the whale

Later, she waded into the ocean
to lay many eggs that
I sprayed with sperms

Now, from the ocean, we watch
the shore receding,
land dwindling,
cities crumbling,
& earth drowning.

The ocean of love gently ripples over them.

A SHOWER OF NIPPLES

In the dark
a nipple bulb switches on—
too hot to touch, it
gently chuckles &
playfully,
switches off
switches on

A nipple gets in my way everywhere—
floats on my tea, leaps out from my shoe,
hides in my brief, & tickles my anus

I go out to the street—
nipples descend from the sky;
black snowflakes

The nipples change colours
red > green > violet
One of them falls on my palm,
runs on the love line—
it's soft, translucent, and gentle,
calmly, it mounts my mount of venus
and vanishes into the wrinkled skin
I watch its journey up a vein
like a small rabbit burrowing,
it reaches my left nipple
which blows up like a balloon

Now, my left nipple is a bbw—*
it seduces men, it fucks men
it seduces women, it fucks women

I graze it gingerly
as it grows under my touch
I explode into a million pixels

*bbw – big breasted woman

IMA UNBORN

*Ima**, ether, sperm of the mist,
brews like wine in her womb
I see her in a vision
                in a crystal orb
        sparking spasmodically

Ima cries beyond the opaque foliage/ garbage heaps,
the stabbing drop of the cliffs/ the glass towers,
the prenatal seas that echo her first howl/ the ambulance wail

Her mother, night's traveller, gentleswayer, seductress,
                                                blood moons rise on her flanks
Her diktat is my fate, a dark star on the rise
Her laughter freezing my image in the pool
Her breath, a twister sucking swan songs in
Her womb, a dragon egg wrapped in grapheme foils

She wields a-
                        guitar
            gun
                        quill
            brush

In bed, under the sheets,
on the windswept wobbling oceanic bed
[where blood runs dark, and words cower in fright]
she draws me firmly into her crater,
crushes me in the vice-grip of her thighs
screams - skewering the dome, the sky, the globe
give me Ima~my~ baby~of~the~fire~spitting~mountains

Then, she
snaps the guitar strings/twang!
shoots me with the gun/bang!
drives the quill into my heart/ugh!
paints me off the earth with her brush/swish!

With the birth of Ima, I am reborn

Ima* - a female baby name

GOD'S BODY YARD

I regret, gal. U been injected with
one shot of
Genuflik Fatero Mortalis fluid
Am not sure, but u'll now go thru a scattering of DNA
putting flora and fauna into ur system

U naked on the chrome table and me observing
ur organs close. There u see changes happening. Ha!

Ur right nipple turns into a green grape
left, into a sweet cherry
Lips are halves of a peach
Nostrils two hibiscus flowers
Eyes, one a blue and the other a red lotus
Ears, two conch shells
Ur neck is a slender giraffe
Belly, a dry lake
Pubic hair, a pine forest
Vulva, a violet apology for an igloo
Clitoris, the Kohinoor
of the great coral reef barrier
Anus, the mouth of a volcano
Bum, two halves of ripe jackfruit

The mutation is a celebration
as the Garden of Eve turns more colourful
& imaginative
The Tree of Knowledge is not just a tree,
but a fish/ a bird/ a reptile/ a toad/
a transman/ woman/ animal
all who wait silently
for the x-beings to evolve

GIRL ON FIRE

I saw her for a fleeting second
in which several molecules
of hydrogen and oxygen mated.
I pressed my lips on hers and
heard a crackle, and rumble.

When I looked back, she was
smiling; a flare began
from her teeth spreading over her tongue
and mouth, and soon her eyes, and
hair were all ablaze.

I ran back to douse the fire;
to save her—every fleshy inch, every cavity,
nerve ending, vessel, organ, cell bacteria
        billowed smoke from her eyes,
ears, nose, nipples, skin, vagina

She was like a hill on fire—
        smelling of roasted birds
                                decayed snakes
                                muted hopes
tattooed swamps, & nightmares

"Don't. Don't. Don't burn," I cried.
She said in several tongues of flame,
                "I am burning to feel the life of trees."

Then I knew
                she was burning from love.

HALF A LIFE WITH A GLUED GIRL

Once I fell in love
with an *ottamulachi** —
a one-breasted woman

I told her,
"Your lovers are scoundrels
eating away the other breast."

She said,
"This one nipple was waiting for you,
half of a pair, half of a cunt, half of a face
half of a heart, half of a soul, half of a life
I only need half of you."

She raised her sword and cleaved me in half.
One half she glued to herself,
and cast away the other to my lovers.
Thus, we became the oddest couple around
withbizarre bodyparts stucktogether.

When one ejaculated, the other menstruated
When one jerked off, the other fingered
When one grunted, the other mewed

We began a long innings of self-love.

*Ottamulachi – Malayalam for one-breasted woman.

MORAL DEATH OF AN ELEVATOR

Walls have eyes/Floors have eyes.
Ceilings have eyes/Corridors have eyes.
Even Loos have eyes.

Fleeing the loony eyes/We run to the Elevator.

Elevators don't have eyes.
We kiss in the Elevator with mirrors
as it carries kissers and huggers
up and down, down and up.

Doors open. Doors close.
Unkissing people come in, go out.
We kiss in the Elevator with mirrors.

One day, the Elevator sprouts an eye
that watches us kissing.
Making love is so good then
as the Elevator trembles throbs and hums
and the mirrors turn concave and convex.

Next day, the Elevator closes in on her
and wants to kiss her through the mirrors.

We dash away to the fire escape.

Evening, the Elevator commits suicide,
crashing down to minus zero level.
A suicide note says,
"Blessed are the kissers
for they are born with lips
that set fire to elevators."

SUMMER RAIN OF THE BREASTS

Everyday
            my lover gives me her breast
            and commands,
                        'Kudi,' 'Kudi,' 'Drink.'
She is large breasted
unlike the small Korean breasts I drool over.
Large hearted too. Large brained.
She forces
            Kaali into my mouth.
(See I have named them Kaali and Neeli,
Black and Blue, though she is pale yellow.)
I turn into little Lord Krishna and
                        she, the illusory Maya.
Glug glug glug blurp glug!

But, Kaali waits impatiently.
I turn into infant Kristu and
                        she, the Virgin.
Glug glug glug blurp glug!

But, these days, her boobs have gone dry.

My toothless gums grate against her dry fruits.
Almonds, chestnuts and currants.
"Rain, dear, wait till the rain"
she croons warmly, tousling my hair.

From Kaali, I squeeze out a few drops of bitter gourd.
From Neeli, some gooseberry.
Before I could suspect some aloe vera, she quotes me playfully,
"They are Fallen Condoms now!"

Ruefully, I wait for the return of the love clouds,
the love monsoon winds,
the love waves,
the love rain.
A small crowd has started gathering
around Kaali and Neeli,
for the spout, the sprout, the fount.
Some crows, squirrels and cats,
even some tendrils of cucumber
and jasmine vines……..

And, love thirsty me.

THE CASE OF THE GIRL WHO CAME BACK

The girl who came back
wasn't the girl who left.
(Is the Spring every year the same Spring?
Don't the vicissitudes fornicate in the green room
to emerge with fabricated DNA prints?)
She wasn't even a girl.
But, the Come Back Girl.
She came back as a Goddess
As a Seductress.

She came back multi-limbed multi-tongued multi-vaginal unisex
multi sex and hyper sexed.

She came back as Sex and Beyond
blowing like a storm on the surface of the Sun.

Wasn't another girl.
Wasn't half the girl.
Wasn't the whole girl.
Wasn't even a girl.
Was, but, the Come back Girl.

On the bed, she grew like a tree,
hopped like a doe,
neighed like a mare,
wriggled like a glow worm,
growled like a tigress,
squealed like a sow
and napped like a rose.

She was the girl, was a girl, wasn't the girl, was the only girl, wasn't a girl at all, wasn't a goddess, wasn't a seductress, wasn't her in whole or parts, wasn't a tree, doe, mare, worm, tigress, sow, rose.

She was my Girl
My Come Back Girl
My Girl beyond touch.

THE NARCISSIST

All his mirrors were women.
They displayed him with breasts
and vaginas and flesh buds.

Desperate,
he approached a blue lake
to see his male splendor.
His cock-a-doodle-do.
His rippling muscles.
His all knowing gaze.
Commanding brow.

The lake called him `Sister!'
and drowned him
in an incestuous
sororal whirl.

SCORING WITH A SOCCER GIRL

Making love to a soccer girl
must be like making love
                                        to earth.

She smells   of grass,
tastes   of mud
                           a little sun heat,
                           a little moon cold
                           a lemony wedge of the sky.
As the ball slices it
            the sweat from worm holes
            the spit of female spiders
            crab flesh from the loins
            fishes from arching knees
            the sap of green caterpillars
            springing hills trapping the ball
            octopus hair shaking the stars free
            the sinews taut and eyes sharp
            like camouflaged panthers

rushing in for the kill/ the goal
the ball juggling from knee to knee
thigh to thigh and river to river
the agonizing cry of a crow pheasant
as the ball curves in from the corner
the little knee jerk fouls, the profanities
rising from missed passes/moves/desires
the headers in the rain
the rolls on the slippery ground
the blood from grazed elbows
the knock out and the deep sleep
on a wavy stretcher to the dressing room
smelling of fresh roses
And spongy leather.

When I try to enter her, she cries
"Offside Offside!"

AN UNDERTAKER LOSES HIS PHONE

I know of a mass grave
where cell phones
go to die.
            One day you may lose one.
            Don't look for it.
            It has buried itself.

Near the swamp
where the secret grave is
the cell phones come out
to play in the night.
      millions   of fireflies,
      million   iridescent organisms,
      million   beeps,
      million   ring tones,
      million   languages.

Some wriggle some fly
some sing some sob.

They come alive
when their loved ones
      call out to them.

            Because love reaches them
            only underground.

DRY RUN

I hate the dryness of things.
Dry kissnesses /wellnesses /sandnesses.

Can I borrow from your soupy mouth
                    the rich saliva lashing in waves
                    in the ocean beneath the ocean,
                              frothy/perfumed/sweet?

Can I worm into your deepest nodes
and suck out the lymph of life?
          Can I dig into your hardiest veins
          and siphon out the plasma of life?
                    Can I crush your finest bones
                    and extract the elixir of life?

Kisses are wet bombs
D r o p p i n g from outer space
on a lake of fire on a loony night.

My wet girl/my wet bomb girl
My girl/my juicyjuicygirl,
          When can I sip from your wounded womb
                    that love, that dream, that other life,
                    that salted bloodliness
                    in your bombed mouthiness?

I am a missile seeking your warmth.
          One touch. We e x p l o d e!

PUSSYLOVE

Each night I discern
in her fanged pelvic isle
a blood yawning cat
juicy moused.

Cat under, puss upon, cat in, puss around,
cat when, puss who, cat where, puss what?
    What's a cat?
    A tale of nine lives / A life of nine tails /
    A tail of nine lies / A lie of nine tales?

The lie that's her isle is a vanishing
pooooooooooooooooooooooocha,*
    Silver by moony night / Quicksilver by sun.

We play cat & mouse year in month out
in disneylandpussylandmousyland
in 4D 5D 9D
        strata spectra spatia
        flipping dimensions,
        entering P / exiting Q.

You, my eternal pussy,   I squeal.
You, my eternal rodent,   she meows.
Her soft footfalls echo silent   in the death chambers.
My shrill squeaks thin out   in the love burrows.

Death / Love / Chamber / Burrow
moans a night cat blackishly.
    I huddle with her in the attic arm chair,
        we barter delicious tongues,
    cat tongues.

*Poocha - Malayalam for Cat

PARALYSIS

Told my toes.
Wake up, brothers, wriggle.
Don't you touch the quickness of her waves?
She is riding them, she is coming.
Wake up,   my numb brother.
Feel the flame   on her tongue
as she engulfs you   in her blushing cheeks.

Told my thighs.
Wake up, brothers, quiver.
Don't you feel the tremor in her gait?
She is striding towards you, she is coming.
Wake up,   my numb brothers.
Feel the lightness   of her wings
as she flutters above   your shaking flesh.

Told my lips.
Wake up, brothers, part.
Don't you taste the rush of her honey?
She is flowing to you,   she is coming.
Feel the sting of her   jasmine teeth
as she pries open the   urn of your mouth.

I discern her on the far horizon.
                She is near.
                She is.
My body groans
and, splutters to life!

THOUSAND WAYS AND ONE WAY TO LEAVE

How does one leave?
By the 9'o clock Town to Town?
12'o clock Shatabdi?
3'o clock Airbus?
By road, rail, air?
How do people leave?
How did she leave?
Stepping across a terminal line of dormant deceit?
Crawling through a glass wall of dashed desire?
Slithering through a membrane of mounting misery?
Sliding through a mirror of tired dejection?
Drilling through a cavern of lost pleasures?
Wading through a sewer of shattered hopes?
Falling through a crater of simmering love?
How did she leave?

This soggy house seeps.
The air is shot with holes.
Did she leave by the cracks in the tiles?
Punctures in the drain pipes?
The dark lizard back alleys?
Gloomy rat race tracks?

Slippery catwalks in the attic?
Winding worm holes in the wood?
Ant holes in the earthen walls?
Labyrinths of termite mud?

How did she leave?

Through the short circuited power cords?
The rat-bitten cables?
The red green amber wires?
The buried optical fibres?
The ever open portals?
How did she leave my world?

How do I?

But, when I spew my bad blood,
I see her stamp on every cell.
And before I could spot her in the scan,
the clot thickens, the wound closes,
she is lost in flesh.

VOLCANO BITES

A toothless mouth
sports the devil's tongue
that slips and slithers into
oyster caves.
Paused and cursed with a crimson prison.
Tongue in cheek
slobbers over a lover and slurps her in
in a froggy meal.

A toothless tongue
is a fleshy candy bar
crazily spicy
that delves deep into little crevices,
caverns, pits, circus rings and sweeps the earth clean
rolling the moon and wiping the stars away.

A toothless mouth
is a long playing record
that broadcasts into subterranean pangs
soaked in acids and enzymes.
Sometimes, it strays too far
into still smoking volcanoes
and pays the price
at the altar of love.

Nailed on the mount
slaughtered on the victory stone
burnt to yellow ash
for volcanoes are toothless
with a nasty bite
and are places where
love erupts into
charred worldly charms.

SHE TAKES WING

She departs, leaves, exits, flies off, decamps, embarks, packs off,
and sets sail.
She takes wing.

Her departure, leaving, exit, flight
brings on an evolution
of neurons, corpuscles and follicles,
transforms the dna, cleans out the plasma
and lays siege to the arteries and lymph nodes.

Done with me, it spreads like a dreaded plague
to the exterior,
wiping the green off the leaves,
rubbing off red from the sun and gold from the moon,
blue from the ocean and black from the dark mystery
nights.
It splits the roads, overturns ships,
brings down the towers and flattens the monuments.

Yes, her departure does all that.

I will see her dancing on the rim of a volcano and

she will see me faltering at the brink of an abyss.
What shall we cross?
        A razor's edge or a wormhole?
        A time-warp on a faulty time-machine?

She stands smiling, holding open the night sky
a foot raised to cross the threshold of asteroids, meteors and
stray space shuttles.
        She is an UFO, an egg, a smooth sperm
        poised to take off into the womb of space.

After she leaves,
                the launch pad will be dismantled.
                The station shut down and sealed.
                The town will be evacuated.
        Google Earth will show a desert
        where I once bloomed.

THE CONTORTIONIST

Loneliness is the whiplash of cold shower/creak of door hinges/groan of gadgets/wing beats of window pigeon/lip rashes on skin/saliva and semen on sheets/shredded notes/coins jingling in brain/fallen hair shampoo smell/throttled tubes of creams.

Loneliness is absence, beckoning abyss.
Loneliness is the ugly fear of the night.
Cold cold cold on a desert bed seeping
through the toes.

You hunt hunt hunt for the warmth warmth
warmth of her. Her smell, on all fours,
her smell on the floor, like a dog, smell
smell smell her on the sheets
on the walls, on the toilet seat,
snout to the ground, twisting, turning,
contorting, looking for her smell
in dusty cavities.

Loneliness is you
who bury your nose into
the deep furrows of your groin
to howl/not to howl when you
find/not find the spoor of love.

LAYER BY LAYER

As delicately as soft petals torn apart
we both unravel

layer by layer

layers of unbridled portals of sporadic passion
layers of windblown pane-broken windows
layers of wavy flower scented stained bed spreads
layers of icy robes drenched in transparency
layers of vaporous skin glistening with sporty sweat
layers of the calcium tautness of brittle bones
layers of the throbbing flesh soaked in fresh frozen
blood
layers of the webby mesh of tubes, tunnels and
wormholes
layers of pure mess, mucus and feces
layers of putrid matter, mind and mindlessness
layers of the flaming dreams
layers of desires
and rays.

Till
with a pitiful roar of the elements in disarray

we fall
layer by layer

to the ground to touch
and germinate the earth.

OCEAN BIRDS

Uncertain birds are dark broodings
that roar past you   tearing away the wings
and stripping the   borders of flags and olive leaves
and gunships   and shells booming like hell.

They traverse a madhouse sky
from which is born   a thick soupy wasteland
chopping and grating the earth into
splinters of   fear, oracles and doom.

Till the moon hurtles through the sky with its entourage
of fallen angels and
          stills the sea to a poisonous blue, a dangerous brew,
          that freezes into a prophetic mirror
          which holds up to you a still life
of motion   as in travel,
of direction   as in a pathway,
of you   as in propagation,
of the bird   as in crossing,
of love   as in a drop of ocean without borders.

PREDATORS

Smelled her
behind her ears and she
squirmed and said: Look
at my breasts! so rounded! my body
so lithesome! my pubis! so pulpy!

Told her:
Wait, let me smell you first before
I perceive you, sense you, hear you, mouth you!
as I smelled you in prehistory like
an olfactory predator!

We, then, smelled each other,
pore by pore, scar by scar, traversing
the longitudes and latitudes of the skin country
across canyons and crevices, pools and peaks,
oyster mouths and misted meadows.
We loved as we loved eons ago
as predators on the prowl
as the hounds and the hunted.

Once every smell was smelled and
Every cell was divided and
every drop of life was fragmented,
we lay exhausted.

And, the world began to smell us.

LOVING ARCHITECTS

They are trendy
concerned with shapes, sizes and curves,
verticality and trajectory
beams and booms

Some like it heavy and solid
like a behemoth, a hill carving,
interiors cut into solid rock,
with sabres rattling inside.

Some live in the clouds
airy and fluffy and bluey
pinky like cotton candy
with plenty of glass and gloss
effortless and floating.

Some like deep hard wood
polished agonizingly
Spsmooth and cool
and resting heavily
on gravitational fields.

I like the bamboo ones
that have fissures that cause the wind to whistle young
that bend and sway never break to the fiercest of winds
that rub each other so frenziedly
that sparks fly and a whole grove is set on fire
in a cleansing way
crackling in ecstacy.
I love architects
who creak
when touched with a quill.

LOVE IN THE TIME OF THROMBOCYTOPENIA

Petechiae bloom
        on a terracota horizon
        as a stylus dipped in copper
        works on the red spots
        star picking coordinates of flesh
among dark wool thickets.

Gradually
        a s(k)in map emerges
                from the land locked sea of memories.

St.Joan bares her
virgin nipples.
        Throbbing thrombocytes
        trickle through
wetting parched gun mouths.

LOVE IN THE TIME OF ANGIOPLASTY

If the god of non-existent desires asks me what I desire to be,
without hesitation, I will say
I want to be a stent in her body
in one of the arteries leading to her heart.

Firmly positioning myself there,
I will watch the passage of corpuscles and molecules, thoughts
and events, kisses and chemical compounds of love, a few stars,
certain violet moons, some sparks of exploding light and galaxies
in demise.

She will never know I am there inside her,
smoothening the creases, dilating the blocks,
swimming in her protoplasm, merging with her genes,
navigating spirals.

When she dies, I will watch her heart decay, her body dissolve.
I will float in some fluid moored to her bones.
Her soul, translucent, will sway above me, her hair
pouring down on me.
She will pick me up gingerly and stick me in her hair bun like a
pin.

That will be the moment I choose to die.

SEXTING IN SLEEP

Girl, if you ask me what happens when a somnambulist sleeps, I will say he sleeps for twenty years and sexts in sleep to his adolescent fantasy women who come alive and start somnambulating in their own little little sleeps.

His fingers jab on the keys as he goes through crests and dips as his libido starts to snore, see, his libido is pre-pubescent and yet to discover semen.

He has visions of Molly teacher's mammaries, Bina teacher's bumz, Nazeema teacher's navel (dreaming secularly) and imagines crashing through soft soapy bushes and watching gopikas bathe, dogs pulling a chain on a bitch near the tar bins, politicians caught on hidden cameras screwing their mistresses, Zeenaths in wet saris, nurses in white, nuns in their habits, an old old poor innocent sexter is he.

At the end of the sexty walk, he wakes up in a texty phone, his phallus lit up like a smarty phone, with shiny buttons waiting to be pressed, its eyes seeing far like a Hubble telescope, locating parts and pieces of a woman body, and in ever growing audio track the texty sexty phallus keeps calling

Oh yeah oh yeah oh yeah! Oh! Girl!

THE GIRL WITH TONSURED HEAD

The girl with tonsured head stops the traffic.
Signals go haywire.
In her wake, electric poles are uprooted,
servers break down,
satellites go blank,
blossoms adorn the foot path,
an inexplicable fragrance blows in the wind.

I was alone at the sea shore waiting for the moon to rise
when the girl with tonsured head rose up from the sea.
In a moment her head turned into a red moon, blue moon
and green moon. Two seas rumbled in her eyes - one opaque
and one translucent.

I passed through her eyes to her brain.
The world shimmered and sparked around me.
I moved from lobe to lobe,
crossed canyons and volcanos,
unknown sounds and unknown colours.

In her head, a universe was being formed,
clots were amalgamating into planets,
two amaeboe were mating and merging,
two goddesses with tonsured heads
were entwined in furious throes.

On a quiet shore
I heard popping sounds.
Pink turtles were laying black eggs.

STARRY STARRY NIGHT

Love is when
you are sick in bed with
hundred and three degrees fever
and she chats in to say
she is sick too
the air vibrates in delirium
and you know it's she coughing
far far far away.

She is cold but your fever
reaches out to warm her lungs.
Kiss is when a scalding tongue
Thaws her frozen mouth.
There is a faint pulse
there is none.

You spoon her
in her far far far bed.
She rolls in your bed
scorched by the heat in your groin
Thus the night passes
Coughing and feverish
wheezing and sweating
four arms touching
and untouching
heat waves rising and falling
dreaming each other.

What a starry starry night!

A SPOONFUL OF SNORES

Snores are dead dreams, said she,
dreams strangulated at birth.

then, she turned to me and pecking my lips, said,
but you only purr! like a cat
after milk,
stork after crab, man
after woman.

Then, she began a series of light snores
darting them at my nape and I thought
of the dreams
we both had killed.

`Spoon me," she whispered and I turned in sleep again.
I dreamt of the soft belly of a whale
I had harpooned once
a mermaid inside her.

Her nipples waxed and waned
and her butts peaked and ebbed
like the tides.

Her snores grew feeble as she died in my arms.
The air grew chilly and we froze like two moons.

I laid my head on her now dead breasts
and heard the faint snore of a
warmly
spooned
heart!

THE ARMPIT NATION

"Thou art b'rn from mine own armpit"
boomed my mom
                    in maharani ingleesh.
I wondered often how!
Since then,
arm pits   have been objects of
                    delicate
                    discreet desire for me.

women conclude I am a pervert
taking a peeko at their
                              boobos.
the truth is I don't inhabit
                              boob country.

armpit is my home ground, cockpit,
                    my nation.
Male gaze theory doesn't work here.
It's less ophthalmic
                              than olfactory.
Male nose theory might work.

nose is just a double barreled prick.
(feminists have to come up with a new hashtag)

One day, I swooned
like the paramahamsa
on watching the swans.
A swan swatted her wings in my lover's armpit
that smelled of sour sweat and trapped breast milk.
(She just had a kid, not mine.)

believe me, when I was a kiddo
an armpit could lift my peppo
from fifty yards away
if the wind was fair.

Told a recent lover
"Crawl into my womb. You will be warm in there."
She said
"your armpit is my womb."
Dug a trench and settled in there.

Wonder if my armpit sprouts
a cunt.
After all, she needs an exit quite soon.

ANDRO AND ESTRO

Androgen and estrogen
met over a cup of energen.
You know how macho
                    Androgen is
and how feminine
                    Estrogen is.

Androgen complained.
These males are horrible.
A little extra of me and
                    they turn
                    rapists.

Estrogen complained.
Same with the women.
A little extra of me and
                    they fall for
                    prince charming.

A riot was on in the city.

A mob came. Jealous of androgen's huge phallus
they   cut   it   off,
                                        leaving him to die
while   watching them   rape estrogen.

Now, this city has vague males
                                        and vague females inhabiting it.
And gender is a confusing concept.
Self fertilization
                              is the in thing.

Emasculated Androgen and
stitched up Estrogen
                                        have fled.
They are said to be living
in an island named
         dopamine.

SOME MEATY THOUGHTS ON LOVE AND ROMANCE

IF you were a tree, I would mount you,
limb to limb,

and shake free all the fruits
slipping and crashing with a broken bough.

IF you were a lake, I would plunge into you, ripple by ripple,
diving down the watery grave
to find a pair of dark eyes open.

IF you were a bulbul, I would strum all strings, in frantic haste,
till the keys grew tremulous with love
singing a requiem sand on sand ash on ash.

But, I am no meat, carbon hydrogen oxygen
no chemical compound no plasma no urea.

Suns and moons, winds and clouds had seeped through our kissing lips in a march of destiny. Satellites and space ships, missiles and gunships had loomed over our writhing selves in orbital fantasies.

Your hair wraps around me
like a jasmine vine.
White fragrance choking me
in a floral hailstorm
A caravan of chameleons make across the glacier
A jammed highway of
red green yellow lights.

My love, if you were a tree,
a lake, a bulbul!
IF I were meat,
not a chewed bone!

WAKING THE CAKE

Cakes are sleepy things; we have to wake
them and eat them
like women,
not that we cannot eat sleeping women.
We can eat women
in any which way we want.
But they are best when baked, like cakes.
Their aroma is divine
when fresh from the oven
The aroma we get
when we spread their legs.
Discerning something like heaven I often ask my girl
and she says, with a smile,
mycakeisbaking.

Finally, I did bake a cake on her smooth belly and oven.
Give you the ingredients.
1 cup white sugar
1/2 cup butter 2eggs
2 teaspoons vanilla extract
1 1/2 cups all-purpose flour
1 3/4 teaspoons baking powder
1/2 cup milk.
Am waiting for her to have a baby

to save on the milk.

Was almost swooning when the rest went well,
You know, the preheating, greasing, creaming, beating,
stirring, combining, mixing, smoothening, pouring,
spooning, then the final baking. Remember,
don't be greedy.
Let things work in their own time.
After all, the cake will be done
only when it springs back to the touch.
and
when she kisses you.

and when the cake crumples between your
bodies,
then you don't use spoons.
You lick the cake from the crevices.
Cake is sin. Cake is sin.
Nevertheless, devour it.

But, make sure it doesn't smell of sulphur.
You may be licking a crater.

MS NEMESIS

I met her
beneath
the palm tree
on a paddy field ridge
in a moonless boneless windless night.
I took her for the local yakshi*
who rode sturdy men and
pickled their
pricks.
But, she declared (in a thunderous voice)
that she was
my nemesis.

Now, this was exciting.
Had heard of this lady, been looking for her
to be sucked dry.

She laughed
(hideously is the word!)
She crooned
(poetically is the word!)

"I am your FIN," she thundered (again).

"Thy show is busted, thou art scrambled. Breathe out your last wish, mortal."

I looked up at the towering palm
and feebly croaked,
"Kallu**! Kallu** Kallu**"

She dragged me to the bushes
and I died the little death
While toddy poured on us
from the palmy
heavens
wetting her buttocks
as they rose and fell.

These days, she makes
a guest appearance
at the loony state asylum
to give me a shot of toddy in the vein.

Her badge catches the sun:
`Ms. Nemesis.'

She whispers in my ears: "Next time,
I'll make you
an eggfruit."

*Yakshi- A legendary female fairy/spirit that charms/seduces men and makes a meal of them. Frequently found on palm trees.
**Kallu – palm toddy

NONCONSENSUAL SEX ON VALENTINE'S DAY

At dawn, she woke up to the clang of utensils from the kitchen.
When she opened the door, they flew out cups saucers ceramic
plates brass pots pressure cookers sauce pans ladles spoons
encircling and kissing her.
Come with us - they cried,
We're making love to you the whole day!
No poaching, roasting, frying, grilling today
We take you apart limb to limb.
Skin to skin.
Follicle to follicle.
Molecule to molecule.
We tire you out with
'Non consensual sex.'
They carried her away to a vast thick cotton white cloud where
they took her one by one.
She grunted like thunder.
Wailed like a sea wind.
Blushed luminescent like a glow worm.

Gushed like a water fall.
Soon, the animate joined the inanimate.
All animals, birds, fishes, flowers made love
to her relentlessly.
Pore to pore.
Cups saucers ceramic plates brass pots pressure cookers sauce
pans ladles spoons
they returned in the evening.
they and the man in the house
waited for her to return.

She never did
never did
never did
But, it did pour for another year
without let without let without let.

SUMMER SNOW

Under water
the sea is purple with the blood of sperm whales
just born.
The bone marrow sticks to the gums plasters the mouth
froth emerging from snorkeling gullets.
A shoal
of sardines
are waiting.

A poignant moment
suspended between high noon and standstill sea
Under water.

Two bodies in death throes.
                    Two octopus arms groping.
                         Two strands of swaying sea weeds.

Slow motion is the mother of Newton as the mouth erupts with
a gush of paraffin, clouds, rings, marsh vapours, smoking gums

Magnesium flares under water
                    rising to the flotilla of mermaids
                              caught in the sky gills
                    spouting like the harpooned whales
Singing in the horizons
seeking the   elusive   fallopian fish.

The first snow falls
                    in her summer mouth.

TRANSLATION

One day, she asked me
to translate her into me.

In return, she offered
to translate me into her.

I began with her toes.
She began with my eyes.

Her toes, I translated
as my vertebrae.
A hot storm blew through my spine
as I sucked each of them.

My eyes, she translated
as her nipples.
Snow fell on her erect peaks as she kissed
my throbbing eye lids.

We kept translating.

Her tongue as my penis.
My nose as her clit.
Her lips as my anus.
My penis as her throat.
Her eyes as my balls.
My fingers as her earlobes.
Her vagina as my tongue.
My mouth as her anus.
Her clit as my tooth.

Fully translated, we lay exhausted on the meadow.

Above us we saw
a stealth jet
translating the sky
and a Hwasong-15
translating the earth.

CREATION

She is the Origin of all Species.
From every breath of hers is born the aves.
From every gait, the fauna.
Every dip, the pisces.
Gesture, the flora.

We make love in Island Galapagos and Lesbos.

I bury my nose in her hair and a mesh of knotted roots
loop their serpent coils around me.
I graze her brow with my lips and a herd of musk deer
leap like nascent bubbles in the forest glade.
I gaze deep into her eyes and a swarm of butterflies
flit around her rainbow lashes.
I fence her scented tongue with my tongue and a mouthful of
soupy sea surges into me bringing fish and algae.

She hovers above me and
covers me with her panting body
like a flotilla of plankton.

Green scents envelop me and a
rainforest engulfs us.
We wake up later in a bird's nest
                    a luminous egg between us.
She nestles close glowing like a touch sensitive sky that trembles,
sparks, emits light and chimes with the wind.

(I am her chosen cell,
          sweet chromosome,
                    pet corpuscle.
I erupt at her command.)

I put my ear to her burrow.
          I hear the rabbits.

BAMBOO

This deluge too will pass
when i find you, sweet mother,
          on a bamboo raft,
          sucking your nipple
                    being toeless.
you are nude, sweet mother,
so am I
          As the bamboos creak a lullaby
                    a remnant song in a water world.
The sun is gentle as the moon, sweet mother
as a ripple begins from us
          and sails with the gulls
               like a shock wave
                    from the epicenter.

God, the Nobel winner, watches us, sweet mother,
          under his microscope
               and chuckles.
His consort
cooks him an aphrodisiac
               in a hollow bamboo.

Note: Hindu mythology has the naked God (male) floating on a banyan leaf sucking his toe in the boundless ocean after the deluge. I give him a sweet mother and a nipple.

IN THE RACE WITH THE SUN

In the race with the sun,
she is one and half hours ahead.
In the race with the moon,
she is one and a half eclipses ahead.
In the race with the Milky Way,
she is one and half stars ahead.

Yes, this girl is good.
Wherever she goes, she carries me along.
Sleeping in her bra-hammock,
or, slipped into her vaginal nest
where I go on a
cunt tour.

The rough terrain that forms her
g-spot,
the warm springs that
drip
drip
drip.
the fleshy hills and vales and caves
where I hunt for magic mushrooms,
climbing all the way north to her cervix,
then
w ho o s h i n g down past the labia
out into the open.

For astronomers, it's a black black black hole.
To me,
a shrine
shrine
s h r i n e.

BANJAARAN

The emerald eyed banjaaran
offers green bangles to me.

Where do you get the glass from?
I ask her, now crystal eyed.

From my tears, says she.
I watch the clear gluey stream.

"Where do you get the green from?"
I ask her, now chlorophyll eyed.

From my milk, says she.
She opens her blouse
and shows two founts
of topaz and sapphire milk.

"Can I live with you," I ask
as she packs her bangles.

"I will come to you," she says
"When your heart spouts a rainbow."

She walks away.
My heart erupts
into ash and coal tar.

BODY OF MY WOMAN

Body of my woman
emitting phosphorescent gases
with a serpent hiss
glowing green and hot over me
like a windswept flame
candles of fat dripping lava
on my seeking organs.

You are my volcano
says me whistling like
a cold arctic snowstorm
blowing from the graves
of extinct flora and fauna.
Your saliva and sweat germinating
a hundred trees through
my sweat pores.

each pant, a rose
gasp, a jasmine
growls, a tamarind grove
moans, a palm forest
each gyration, a lunar tide
each bite, a new spouting spring.

You go on tattooing an eden garden
on me, in me, around me.

Body of my woman
crucified on me
buried with me.

ME, MY WIFE AND THE OTHER.

(Confessions of a rotten husband)

Wife cooks, feeds, cooks, feeds
makes my bed, serves me meals in bed.
I crave the other.

Wife bathes me, cleans my bum
washes my clothes, dries and folds them
I crave the other.

Wife shops, buys fish, buys eggs
sends and collects courier packs
I crave the other.

Wife checks my fever,
panics at every cough, every sneeze
I crave the other.

Wife waits outside ICUs
puts up with my tantrums
buys all my medicines

I crave the other.

Wife sweeps, mops,
leaves the floors squeaky clean
deodorizes the toilet
boils water for my daily shave
guards me from dawn to dusk
prays to the Gods, offers them money
removes any discomfort
any wrinkle, any sprain
I crave the other.

I crave the other in the wife.
I crave the wife in the other.
I crave the other in the other.
I crave the wife in the wife.
I crave the wife and the other
in the other and the wife.
I crave the other and the wife
in the wife and the other.

THE RETURN

exiting my secure home
i landed in a suburban train
that took me beyond the city.
the city was fleeing from the city.
the malls, hotels, flyovers, cine houses,
were all fleeing, overtaking the train.
        people were fleeing from people.

on return, i found the city denuded.
no slums no city centers no aerodromes.
the pools and ponds remained and the parks.
        the station stood in a vast marshy land.

when i got off, the lone traveler,
i saw two people lost in a deep kiss.
then her train arrived and
        she alighted all smiling.
the whole station now was steeped in her fragrance.
each empty train, each empty food stall
each empty platform, each empty counter.

hand in hand, we marched off to the marshes
        which soon began to smell of her.

TWO BATH TUB REVOLUTIONARIES

"Come, let's make revolution",
she said
sliding
into the bath tub.
I watched the blood rising in bubbles
from her painted slit beneath her bush.
Slowly, the water was turning red
as she splashed around laughing.
I took out my gun, slid it under her bum
and lay atop her in the warm tub.
Her gun stuck out
from her cunt lips.

Warm water has a way of
turning you to fluid
and two bodies in water
f l o w e d into the other.
I pulled the plug and
water gushed out,
our bodies rising from the sea of blood
like two new archipelagoes making love.

I drew out a bloodied raven

from her womb
and sent it forth in search of
liberated land.
By then doors began to crash open in the tub
and men in green
poured in from each crack.
I shot clock-wise and she shot in reverse
till an army of
green ants
lay dead around.

Only we were left and
we
shot
at
each other.

I ejaculated
when her shot found my heart.
She went into the throes of her deathly orgasm.
'Revolution'
as the installation got titled
looked enchanting in all shades of red.

Our last fading vision was that of a red raven flying back
to roost on us
and caw in terror,
"Long live the Revolution."
My prick
and her clit
stood up in attention.

THE RENDEZVOUS

After the initial tremors of rapture
I examined her body   with a male gaze.
There are two additional tiers I said
                                        looking at her belly.
Yes, she agreed, not just MRF.
Feels like Dunlop, I said.
                        She inflated
                        and deflated.

I went for Kaali, the ever shy one.
            She was sleeping on an upper tier.
            I rudely woke her up
                        with a vigorous lick and bite.
                        She yelped and swayed away.

Where's Neeli I demanded.
            Neeli stooped stubborn in a corner
            refusing to shake hands.

The only unchanged pliant ones
were the ear lobes
          in flesh and blood.
                    Took hours with them in the
                    water theme parks, haunted caves
                    where kids run after rabbits.

Her lips spoke an ancient tongue
          and the tongue a celestial one.
In turn she turned a sniffer dog
          seeking the hidden bombs in my body.

Thus time meandered on its way
till a countable number of tears
sprang from our eyes.

We cried in unison, "We will never meet again."
          We heard a far off rumble.
          It was a volcano erupting
          Along
          the sun's rim.

LOVE IN THE ARMPIT

Mere bhole bhaale sayyan, my innocent lover,
croons she as she begins to unshirt me.
The garbage of the universe is swept away
by a cosmic gastric gale as her nostrils quiver
and test the air and like a diving kingfisher
dive deep into my armpit.

The impact is deafening and I lose my power of speech as her nose digs in and inhales deep for that most exquisite of smells- the whiff of the armpit, the paradise of perfume, the Kilimanjaro of aroma, the Shangri-La of scents.

She comes up for air and mouth open with
undigested dreams
takes the air deep into her lungs with particles
of love and light.
Her nose ridge, nose flesh and nostrils quiver with the moisture
of honeyed sweat.
Ahhhhhh
she says, and
as if in a slow orgasm
dips her head once again
into that cave of solitude, departure, sadness, wetness
and darkness.
Into that realm of burnt candles of unattained love.
Into that realm of incenses burning before a cross.
She dips her nose once again
and inhales
That chloroform of love and death.

When I remove her head
from that lair of lust
she is asleep and
I kiss her sweat-laden mouth
salty from the sweat,
sweet from the nectar.

I let her sleep for a long time till she
comes alive in another birth,
me still beside her
and my inviting armpit.

COUNTING MOLES ON A STARRY SKY

Shimmering like a glow worm after sex,
she lay iridescent, emitting rays and
asked me – sugar, do you count stars
on a starry night cloudless and pure,
the star dust as they descend like
mist on a dark hill? Do you locate
the whorls, whirlpools, comets,
budding infant stars and the dying ones
as they dissipate their last gaseous breaths,
gasps, flames, molecules and atoms?

I replied – yes yes and yes, I do.
Let me start with the moles on your face.
I touched each mole as I counted them
on her eye lids, upper lips, lower lips, filtrum.
I kissed each mole I preferred, or licked them
or merely touched or counted them with my breath.
She shivered slightly as I kept counting
on her nude self still warm to my touch
offering each part of her body with a sigh.
Ten, eleven, twelve…I reached her armpits.

As if to part her hair and count the stars, I lingered
breathing her in as blood rushed madly within me.
Upper breasts, under breasts, lower breasts,
the narrow canyon between her breasts,
as her nipples raised their heads and watched.
Twenty three twenty four twenty five twenty six,
then I smelled her pussy and wondered amazedly
    how many moles, stars, comets, suns
    must be hidden in her folds under her
    moistening hair. I panted and stopped
    asking her to turn over in a shivering voice.

She turned over and her hair covered her back.
I parted her hair and my heart stopped.
There, spread before me, was the splendor
of a clear starry sky till my eyes could behold
till the horizon till eternity, filling the infinite space
with comets, stars, planets, asteroids, black holes and worm
holes, stars in the womb and giant collapsing stars,
all on her glistening back shivering in anticipation,
    a universe in the making.

THE MALADY OF LOVE AND ITS REMEDY

Welcome to the Anti Love Virus hospital
treating love and cloned simulations of it.

As the Hospital PRO, let me bluntly inform your dear selves that Love is an infectious disease spread by a Virus that entered earth's stratosphere with a falling asteroid that killed many species. Love, therefore, is medically treated as an inherently undesirable condition in any human.

Now, look at this state of the art machine that identifies the presence of any form of the Love virus by
Myopic Heliographic Hyacynthixian Corrulo Resonance System.

The machine not only identifies and locates the Virus but also issues veiled threats to it to leave the system.

Most viruses would prefer to evacuate following the Geneva Convention Rule No 0.00.000.001.0001.

Those who don't agree are removed through surgical strikes. Those that still don't perish are tortured every day in public in a specially designed semi transparent hydro tube of heat sensitive Krotium Collodium alloy that can heat the virus from Minus 2 K
to K plus in one minute flat
thus eradicating it forever
with no chance of reincarnation.

This is a spectacular show of rainbow colours much loved
by the loving couples in the audience who hold hands with
surgical gloves and kiss through the surgical masks
their disinfected hearts wrapped in surgical gauze.

MERMAID- AN AMPHIBIAN ROMANCE

Scene 1 / Day /Int- Ext/ Washing machine

Glass eyed, a mermaid swims in my washing machine,
round and round swirls she,
till rescued and spun in the dryer and hung to dry
forked tail clipped, tears dripping from her
ever open eye, detergent from her raven hair.
A sad, wet, fish is she.

Scene 2 /Day-Night/ Int / Bath tub

Brooding over her past, pondering her future
I stand dazed as she grows in my arms.
Soapy rainbows ripple on her belly her scales
drop her tail makes way to two smooth columns
her sex blooms like a hibiscus her breasts swell
her lungs draw in the stale air and exhale the fresh
her lips quiver nostrils quiver eyes quiver hair strands quiver

As she becomes a woman
we spend the night in the bath tub
where she smells of antediluvian fish
and wood borne ancient voyages
across a sea before land was born,
air before the sea was born
and the sky before air was born.

Scene 3/ Day/ Ext/ Beach

I wake to the smell of rotting fish and fish blood and fish entrails.
I trace her to the deserted beach; her tail split apart, her fins broken,
gills filled with filth and fluids of men secreted like spit on the agony
of an amphibian existence.

Take me to the sea, she wails
and I carry her
into uncertain waves,
take her home.

Scene 4/ Day(?)/ Night (?)/ Ext(?)/ Under the sea

in a sunless night, on phosphorescent sand strewn with
shiny bones of animal souls at the bottom of the southern seas,
we consummate our marriage,
I become a merman.

Scene 5/ No Day/ No Night / No Int/ No Ext / No earth/ Voice over

"One day, we will come ashore when
mankind is wiped off the face of this earth
and spawn our half men/ half women
in virgin sand."

THE END

ODE TO YOUR BUNGA

Your *bunga*
is a ripe roasted banana split-
wrapped in red hot coals and ants.

Your *bunga*
is a slit green bamboo shoot-
soaked in cool pools of sap and moons.

Your *bunga*
is the cavern of rattling echoes
where batwings lick the rock salt.

Your *bunga*
is the ripped honeycomb
spurting amber gemstones and angry bees.

Your *bunga*
is the crater of a placid lake
where a blue boat rocks
fading in a sulphur mist
in a splash of moss green.

Your *bunga* is

Shangri-La.

Other Titles by

RLFPAEDITIONS

Brass Neck by *Victoria Naa Takia Nunoo*
En Body by *Meera Nair*
Best Indian Poetry 2018, Edited by *Linda Ashok*

Betel Nut City by *Shalim Hussain*
Teaching Father how to Impregnate Women by *Soonest Nathaniel*
Mother Tongue: Apologize by *Preeti Vangani*

Somewhere but not here by *Stephen Byrne*
Apostrophe by *Barnali Ray Shukla*
The Land below Water by *Manik Sharma*

Available on
rlpoetry.org

www.ingramcontent.com/pod-product-compliance
Lightning Source LLC
LaVergne TN
LVHW091618170726
843492LV00007B/2484

* 9 7 8 8 1 9 3 9 2 9 5 8 2 *